Collins

Easy Learning

KS3 Science Workbook

Levels 3-6

Patricia Miller

About this book

This book has been written to help you prepare for your Key Stage 3 Science Test at the end of Year 9. It contains all the practice you need to do well in the two written papers.

The book is divided into six Key Idea sections (e.g. Cells), which correspond to The Framework for Teaching Science Years 7, 8 and 9. Each double page contains SAT-style questions on a specific topic. At the back of the book there is a practice paper and a revision checklist.

The questions have been given approximate National Curriculum levels to show you what level the question is. You still need to practise answering the lower level questions to check that you fully understand the topic, even if you are working at a higher level.

How to check your answers

You can check your answers for FREE by visiting **www.collinseducation.com/easylearning** where full mark and level guidance is also given in an easy-to-download format.

Revision and practice

Each double page in this book is specifically matched to a double page in Collins *Easy Learning KS3 Science Revision Levels 3–6*. You can revise the topic in the revision book and then test yourself by answering the questions in this workbook.

Published by Collins
An imprint of HarperCollins*Publishers*
77–85 Fulham Palace Road
Hammersmith
London W6 8JB

Browse the complete Collins catalogue at
www.collins.co.uk

© HarperCollins*Publishers* Limited 2006

10 9 8 7 6

ISBN-13 978-0-00-723358-8
ISBN-10 0-00-723358-2

Patricia Miller asserts her moral right to be identified as the author of this work.

British Library Cataloguing in Publication Data
A Catalogue record for this publication is available from the British Library

Written by Patricia Miller
Edited by Mitch Fitton
Design by Graham Brasnett
Illustrations by Kathy Baxendale, Jerry Fowler, David Whittle
Printed and bound by Martins the Printers

Contents

Cell structure

1 Label the diagrams of plant and animal cells.

Plant cell

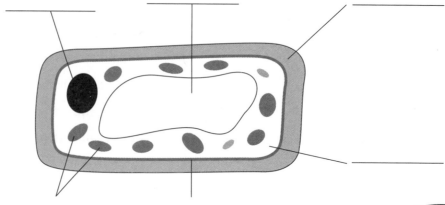

6 marks

Animal cell

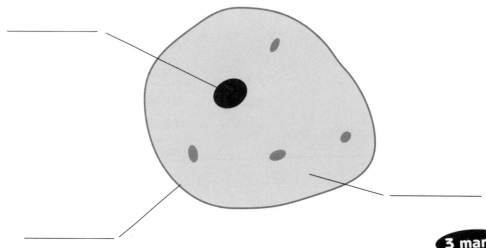

3 marks

2 Which **three** structures do both plant and animal cells have?

a _____

b _____

c _____

3 marks

3 Which **three** structures do only plant cells have?

a _____

b _____

c _____

3 marks

4 Match the part of the cell to its function.

| Nucleus | | Helps keep plant rigid |

| Cell wall | | Matter that makes up most of the cell and where chemical reactions take place |

| Vacuole | | Controls what goes in and out of cell |

| Cell membrane | | Contains green pigment chlorophyll |

| Chloroplast | | Controls chemical reactions in cell |

| Cytoplasm | | Holds water to keep cytoplasm up against cell wall |

5 marks

5 Why do only plant cells have chloroplasts?

_____

_____

1 mark

6 Why do all cells need a cell membrane?

_____

_____

1 mark

1 The diagrams show two different types of plant cell.

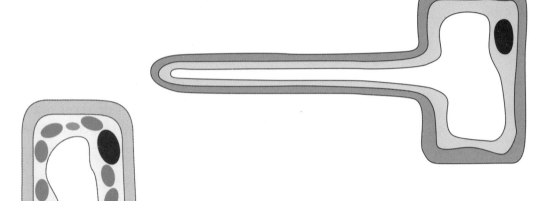

   a Which structure is missing from the root hair cell?

_____

1 mark

   b Why do root hair cells not need these structures?

_____

2 marks

   c In what other way is a root hair cell adapted to its function?

_____

1 mark

2 These cells have adaptations to help them carry out their function.

Sperm cell

Egg cell (ovum)

   a Name **one** adaptation that both cells have.

_____

   b Name **one** adaptation that only an egg cell has.

_____

2 marks

3 These cells both have unusual shapes that help them to carry out their function.

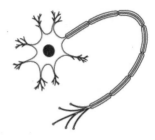

Cell A   **Cell B**

a Which types of cells are these?

Cell A _____

Cell B _____

2 marks

b For cell A

  i In what way is its shape unusual?

  _____
  _____

1 mark

  ii How does this shape make it better at carrying out its function?

  _____
  _____

1 mark

c For cell B

  i In what way is its shape unusual?

  _____
  _____

1 mark

  ii How does this shape make it better at carrying out its function?

  _____
  _____

1 mark

levels
4-5

A   B   C   D

1 a Put the diagrams into the correct order for showing cell division.

_____

_____

b When a group of similar cells join together, what do they form?

_____

_____

2 a What are the **seven** characteristics of living things?

_____

_____

_____

_____

_____

_____

_____

_____

b Which of these characteristics takes place in all systems in the body?

_____

c Name **one** organ that is needed to allow each of these characteristics to be carried out in humans.

Excretion _____

Nutrition _____

2 marks

d i Which organ in plants allows them to make their own food?

_____

1 mark

ii Which characteristic of living things are plants showing by doing this?

_____

1 mark

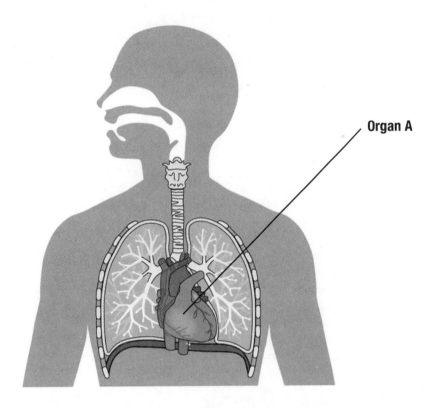

Organ A

3 a This organ is essential to which characteristic?

_____

_____

1 mark

b What kinds of tissue make up this organ?

_____

_____

2 marks

c What do we call a group of organs working together to carry out a particular function?

_____

1 mark

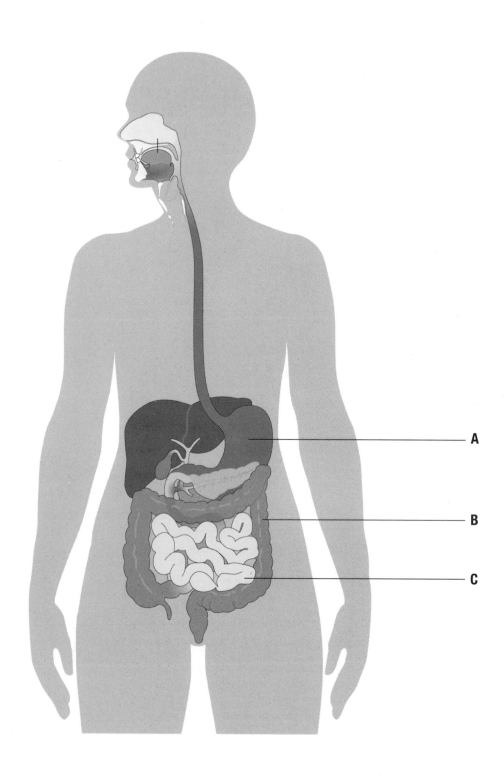

A

B

C

1 a What are the names of organs A, B and C?

_____

_____

_____

3 marks

b Put the correct letter next to the function of each organ given below.

   i The food being digested is broken down into small molecules that can pass through the wall of this organ into the bloodstream.

   Organ _____

   ii This organ has muscular walls to churn up the food.

   Organ _____

   iii This organ is where the final stage of digestion happens and water is absorbed back into the body.

   Organ _____

3 marks

2 a The body produces chemicals to help break down food.
What are they called?

_____

1 mark

b Another one of these chemicals is produced by glands in the mouth.
What is the name of the fluid that contains this chemical?

_____

1 mark

3 a The body uses the energy from digestion in **three** ways – what are they?

_____

_____

_____

3 marks

b Protein is particularly important for **one** of these uses.
Which is it?

_____

1 mark

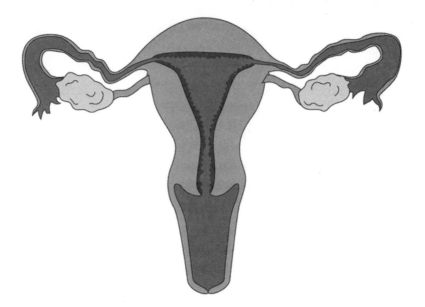

1 **a** On the diagram above, label the organ in which a foetus grows.

1 mark

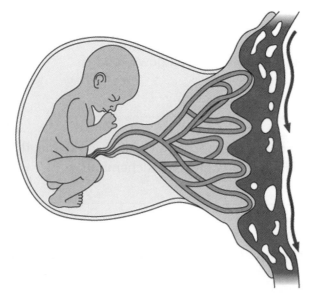

b On the diagram above, label the organ through which the mother passes nutrients to the unborn baby.

1 mark

c Why should a pregnant woman not smoke cigarettes or drink alcohol?

_____

_____

2 marks

_____

2 a How often does an adult female release an ovum from one of her ovaries?

_____

1 mark

b What is the correct term for the release of an ovum?

_____

1 mark

c What happens before this to prepare the uterus for a fertilised ovum?

_____

_____

_____

1 mark

d What happens if fertilisation does not take place?

_____

_____

_____

2 marks

e All the above are stages in a cycle – what is the name of that cycle?

_____

1 mark

f In what way is an ovum adapted to carry out its special role?

_____

_____

_____

1 mark

g How long does a human foetus remain in its mother's body before it is ready to be born?

_____

1 mark

The circulation system

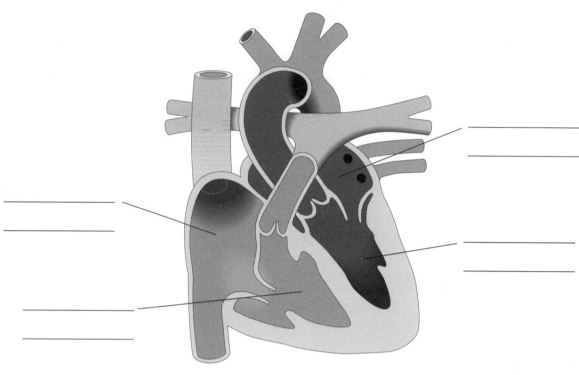

1 a Label the diagram of the heart.

      4 marks

  b Show with an arrow on the diagram which side of the heart sends blood to the lungs.

      1 mark

  c In which side of the heart would you find oxygenated blood?

      1 mark

_____

  d Explain your answer.

_____

_____

_____

      2 marks

2 a Which type of blood vessel carries blood away from the heart?

      1 mark

_____

  b How is this vessel adapted to this function?

_____

_____

_____

      2 marks

3 Put these terms in the correct order to show how an animal or plant is made up.

tissue	organism	cell	system	organ

_____

_____

_____

_____

_____

5 marks

4 a Explain the difference between respiration and breathing.

_____

_____

_____

_____

_____

4 marks

b Explain why your heart beats faster when you exercise.

_____

_____

_____

_____

3 marks

level
4

1 Explain why there is a green plant at the start of every food chain.

_____

_____

2 marks

2

a In the diagram of a cell in the leaf of a plant, label the part of the cell needed for photosynthesis.

1 mark

b What sort of plant cells will not contain this structure?

_____

1 mark

c Explain your answer.

_____

_____

_____

1 mark

3 a What **two** chemicals does a plant need to take in for photosynthesis?

_____

_____

2 marks

b What gas is released as a result of photosynthesis?

_____

1 mark

c Write the chemical reaction for photosynthesis as a word equation.

_____

_____

3 marks

4 A gardener planted some shrubs that grew to be very dense with lots of leaves on the branches. As they grew bigger he noticed that there was a patch of bare earth under each one where there used to be grass. Explain what had happened.

_____

_____

_____

2 marks

5 Explain why plants give out carbon dioxide in the dark and release oxygen in the light.

_____

_____

_____

_____

3 marks

1 a Tick the correct boxes to show which of these are fossil fuels.

Coal ☐

Biomass ☐

Uranium ☐

Oil ☐

Natural gas ☐

Solar power ☐

3 marks

b Are fossil fuels renewable or non-renewable?

_____

1 mark

c Explain your answer.

_____

_____

_____

2 marks

2 a Which gases are released into the environment when fossil fuels are burned?

_____

_____

2 marks

b What harm does each of these gases do?

_____

_____

_____

_____

2 marks

c Which gas that is released when fossil fuels are burned is also given off when biomass is burned?

_____

1 mark

4 Put the following statements into the correct boxes in the table.

A Will one day run out and it is not possible to make more.

B Supplies can be fairly easily replaced.

C Can be used anywhere and when burned gives off a large amount of heat.

D Although not a fossil fuel, still gives off greenhouse gases.

E Can only be used where the conditions are right.

F Is clean to use and renewable.

Energy source	Advantage	Disadvantage
Coal		
Wind power		
Biomass		

6 marks

5 a What is the ultimate source of the Earth's energy?

_____

1 mark

b How can this energy source be used directly?

_____

_____

_____

1 mark

c What is the disadvantage of using this direct energy source?

_____

_____

_____

1 mark

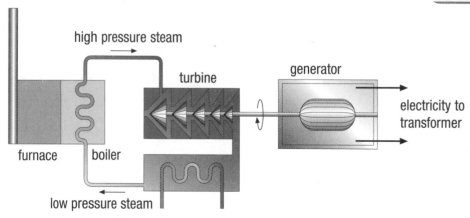

high pressure steam

turbine

generator

electricity to transformer

furnace   boiler

low pressure steam

1 a Put these statements into the correct boxes to complete the flow chart to describe the process of generating electricity using a fossil fuel.

A The steam turns a turbine.

B Fuel is burned in a furnace to release energy in the form of heat.

C The turbine turns a magnet inside a generator which produces the electricity.

D The heat from the furnace heats the water in the boiler which creates steam.

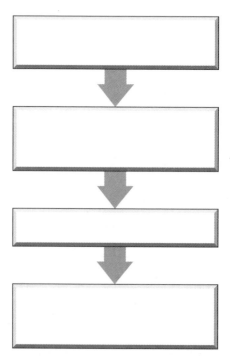

4 marks

b Which part of this process is not needed to generate electricity using wind or wave power?

1 mark

2

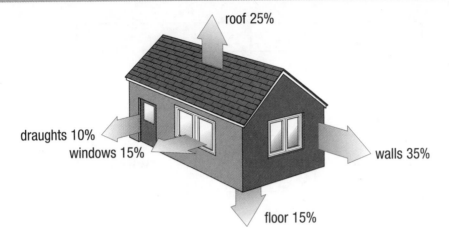

roof 25%

draughts 10%
windows 15%

walls 35%

floor 15%

a Draw a bar chart to show how much heat is lost from this house in each way.

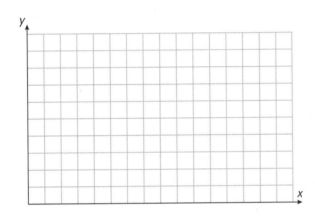

6 marks

b Choose **three** ways in which we can reduce the heat lost from our homes by deciding whether these statements are true or false:

i We can reduce heat loss from our homes by having a shower not a bath. **TRUE/FALSE**

ii Double glazed windows will reduce the heat lost from our homes. **TRUE/FALSE**

iii Loft insulation will reduce heat lost from our homes. **TRUE/FALSE**

iv We can reduce heat loss from our homes by only boiling the amount of water we need in a kettle. **TRUE/FALSE**

v Using energy efficient light bulbs will reduce the heat lost from our homes. **TRUE/FALSE**

vi We can reduce the heat lost from our homes by insulating the cavity walls with foam. **TRUE/FALSE**

6 marks

c The statements which are FALSE are all examples of:

A Money saving tips?

B Ways to cut down on our use of energy?

C Ways to make our homes safer? _____

1 mark

Electrical circuits

levels
3-5

1 Match the symbol to the name of the component.

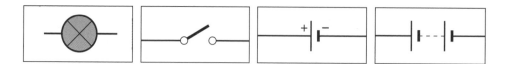

cell	battery	bulb	switch

4 marks

2

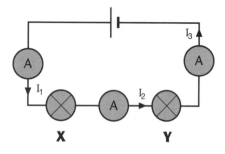

a What do you know about the current at each point in this circuit?

_____

_____

_____

1 mark

b What would happen to bulb X if bulb Y went out?

_____

1 mark

3

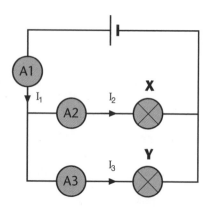

a Which **two** ammeters would have the same reading?

_____

_____

1 mark

b What would the reading on the third ammeter be?

_____

c What would happen to bulb X in this circuit if bulb Y went out?

_____

_____

_____

4 In each of these circuits there is no current – the ammeter reading is zero.

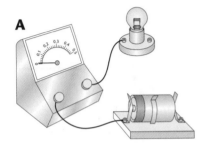  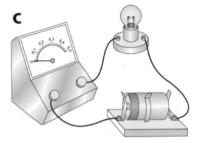

a What is wrong with each of the circuits?

   A _____

   B _____

   C _____

b Draw a circuit diagram for a circuit containing these components that would allow the current to flow.

1 What sort of energy is always present during energy transfers?

_____

2 Why can sound energy not travel through a vacuum?

_____

_____

3

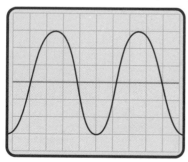

a Draw a wave to show a sound with the same pitch that is much quieter.

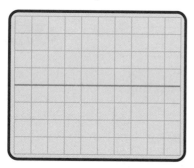

b Draw a wave to show a sound that is just as loud but with a lower pitch.

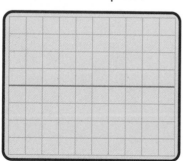

4

a What form of stored energy does this book have while it is still on the high shelf?

_____

1 mark

b What form of energy will it have if it falls?

_____

1 mark

c What forms of energy will this become when the book hits the ground?

_____

_____

1 mark

5 a Which of these stores of energy is the odd one out?

A Food we eat ☐

B Petrol for the car ☐

C The string in a bow and arrow ☐

D The wax of a candle ☐

1 mark

b What form of potential energy is stored in the others?

_____

1 mark

1 A TV set takes in electrical energy from the mains supply.

a What does it transfer this energy as?

_____

_____

_____

3 marks

b Which form of energy is the one that is not wanted?

_____

1 mark

2 a Which of these materials would you choose to make a saucepan from?

wood	glass	aluminium	plastic	copper

_____ and _____

2 marks

b Explain your answer.

_____

_____

_____

2 marks

c Explain why you should always stir a pan of hot liquid with a wooden spoon not a metal one.

_____

_____

2 marks

3 a Why do kettles have the heating element at the bottom? (You should use the word convection in your answer.)

_____

_____

_____

b By what method is thermal energy transferred through a vacuum?

_____

c When a hot cup of tea cools down, how is the heat from the tea transferred to the surroundings?

_____

_____

_____

4 Which of these statements about energy are true and which are false?

a Energy is not created or destroyed, it is just transferred from place to place.   **TRUE/FALSE**

b Energy is sometimes used up, such as when a battery runs out.   **TRUE/FALSE**

c When energy is transferred, it is not always in the form that we want.   **TRUE/FALSE**

d Most of the energy transferred by a light bulb goes into lighting the surroundings.   **TRUE/FALSE**

e Energy is measured in units called joules – this unit is named after a person.   **TRUE/FALSE**

1 What sort of organism is always at the start of every food chain?

_____

2 a What is the name of the chemical reaction that releases the energy from our food?

_____

b Write a word equation for the chemical reaction.

_____

_____

c What do our bodies use that energy for?

_____

_____

3

A

B

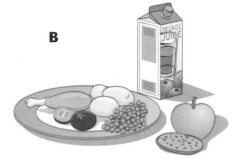

Look at the two meals A and B above.

a Which one is higher in fat?

_____

b Which one is higher in carbohydrate?

_____

c Which one is higher in sugar?

_____

d Which one is higher in vitamins and minerals?

_____

e Which of these meals would you recommend to someone wanting to follow a healthy balanced diet?

_____

f Explain your answer.

_____

_____

_____

_____

2 marks

4 Choose the most suitable intake of energy from food for each person from the box below.

4000 kcal	3000 kcal	1500 kcal	2000 kcal

Person | **Energy intake**

a An adult female with an office job who sits at a desk all day.

b An adult male who works at a hard manual job.

c A pregnant woman who leads a busy active life.

d A 10-year-old boy who plays a lot of sport.

4 marks

5 Labels on food always show the energy content per 100 g. Explain why energy values are shown in this way.

_____

_____

_____

1 mark

Sound and light

1 Complete these sentences using words from the box.

| frequency | loud | pitch | amplitude | high |

It is possible to tell what a sound will be like by looking at the wave.

If the wave has a high _____ then the sound will have

a _____ pitch. The _____ of the

wave tells us whether it will be loud or quiet.

3 marks

2 a Which of these sounds would have a higher pitch...

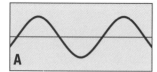 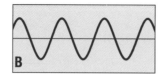

A or B?

_____

1 mark

b ...and which of these sounds would be louder...

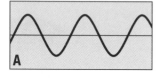 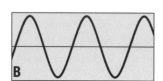

A or B?

_____

1 mark

3 a What name do we give to objects that give off their own light?

1 mark

_____

b Draw lines to match the name to the definition.

Translucent	Lets all the light through
Transparent	Lets no light through at all
Opaque	Lets some light through

3 marks

4

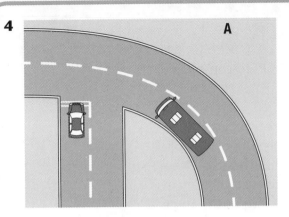 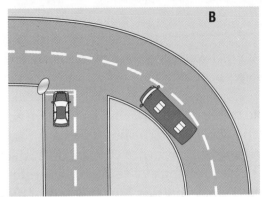

a Mark on diagram A the point when the driver of the car would be able to see the bus coming along the road without the mirror.

b Mark on diagram B the point when the car driver can see the bus coming with the mirror in place.

5 Which of these statements about sound and light are true and which are false?

a Sound and light both need a substance to travel through.   **TRUE/FALSE**

b Light travels about a million times faster than sound.   **TRUE/FALSE**

c Light and sound both travel as waves, moving energy from place to place.   **TRUE/FALSE**

d Older people are better at hearing high-pitched sounds than younger people.   **TRUE/FALSE**

e The Moon gives off its own light.   **TRUE/FALSE**

f We see objects when light from them is reflected into our eyes.   **TRUE/FALSE**

6 Explain why astronauts on the Moon need radios to talk to each other.

_____

_____

_____

Reflection, refraction and seeing colour

1 Circle the correct word or phrase from the choices in bold to complete these passages about light.

We are able to see objects because light is **reflected/refracted** into our eyes. The angle at which light strikes a surface is called the angle of **reflection/angle** of incidence. The angle at which light is reflected from a surface is called the angle of **reflection/angle** of incidence. The angle of reflection is always **half as big/the same/twice as big** as the angle of incidence.

White light is a mixture of **three/seven/ten** colours and objects that look white reflect **all/some/none** of these colours. Objects that look black reflect **all/some/none** of the colours of the spectrum and objects that look coloured reflect **all/some/none** of the colours. Although light always travels in straight lines, it will change direction at the boundary between two substances. This is called **reflection/refraction**. This can make water look **deeper/shallower** than it really is.

2 Put the colours of the spectrum into the correct order. The first one has been done for you.

GREEN	RED	VIOLET	ORANGE
BLUE	YELLOW	INDIGO	

1 RED _____

2 _____

3 _____

4 _____

5 _____

6 _____

7 _____

3 What makes a red traffic light look red?

_____

_____

3 marks

4 Complete the diagrams to show how the ray of light behaves in each one.

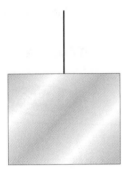  

3 marks

5 Which colours of light are being reflected by these objects when viewed in white light?

a A white shirt

_____

1 mark

b A black coat

_____

1 mark

c A red car

_____

1 mark

1 Which of these statements about forces are true and which are false?

a When the forces on an object are balanced, the object will always be stationary. **TRUE/FALSE**

b Forces can make things change shape, speed or direction. **TRUE/FALSE**

c If an object is moving and the forces on it are balanced, it will continue to move at the same speed in the same direction. **TRUE/FALSE**

d Pressure is greater if the force acts over a greater surface area. **TRUE/FALSE**

e Tractors have wide tyres to stop them sinking into the ground. **TRUE/FALSE**

5 marks

2

This person is pushing down on the chair with a force of 650 N. What other force is acting to make this balanced?

_____

1 mark

3

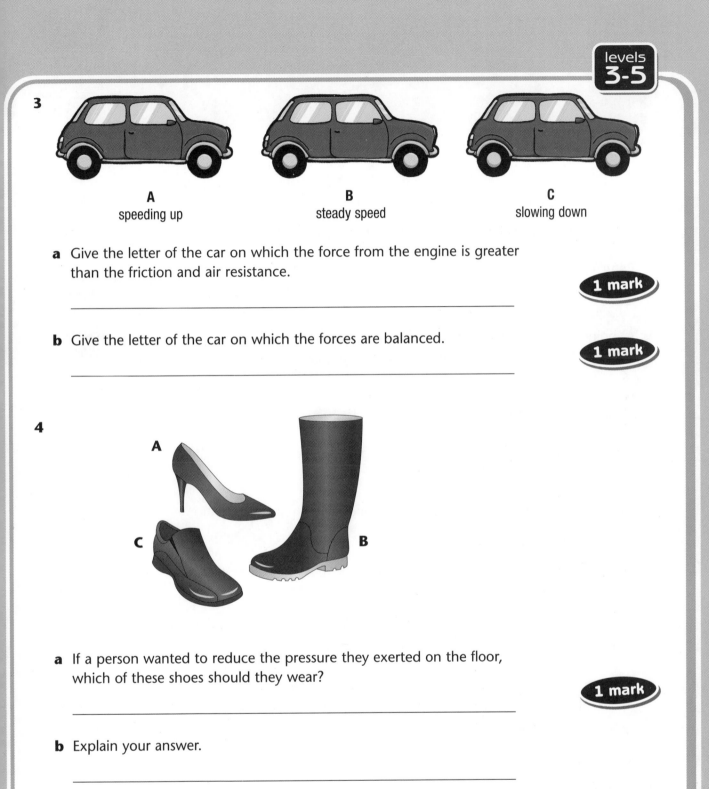

| **A** | **B** | **C** |
| speeding up | steady speed | slowing down |

a Give the letter of the car on which the force from the engine is greater than the friction and air resistance.

1 mark

_____

b Give the letter of the car on which the forces are balanced.

1 mark

_____

4

a If a person wanted to reduce the pressure they exerted on the floor, which of these shoes should they wear?

1 mark

_____

b Explain your answer.

_____

_____

2 marks

_____

1

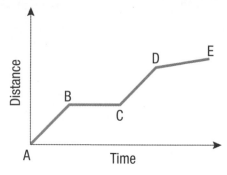

This is a graph of distance against time for a train journey.

a Between which **two** points was the train standing still in a station?

_____

b At point E, the train arrives at its destination station. On the graph, continue the line for the next unit of time.

2 Sarah set off to walk to school. This is how her journey went:

A For 5 minutes she walked quite quickly to get to the corner, where she met her friends.

B One friend was late so the others chatted and waited for 3 minutes for her to arrive.

C They then set off together and walked quite slowly as there was a lot to talk about.

D After 10 minutes Sarah looked at her watch and saw that they were going to be late. They walked very quickly for the last 5 minutes.

E At the school gate they saw they were not late after all so they walked slowly to their classroom, which took another 2 minutes.

On the axes below, sketch the graph of Sarah's journey.

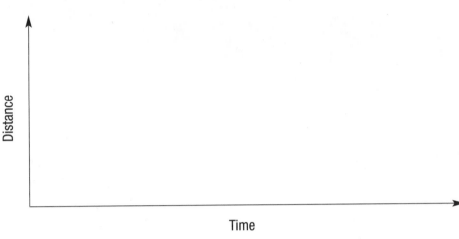

5 marks

3 Choose values from the box to complete the table below.

100 s	9000 m	50 km/h

Speed	Distance	Time
	250 km	5 h
15 m/s	1500 m	
30 m/s		300 s

1 mark

1 mark

1 mark

4 a If a car travels 20 miles in 40 minutes, what is its average speed?

_____

_____

_____

2 marks

b If the car then continues at the same average speed for another 60 minutes, how far will it travel in that time?

_____

_____

_____

2 marks

levels
5-6

1

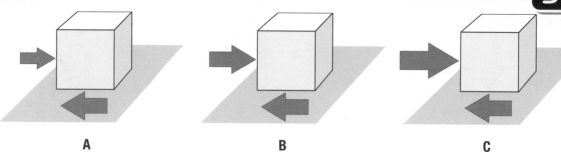

A   B   C

a Which of these boxes would start to move?

_____

2 marks

b In which directions would they move?

_____

_____

2 marks

c Explain your answer.

_____

_____

1 mark

2

a From the picture above, identify **one** place where friction is useful.

_____

1 mark

b Identify **one** place where friction will need to be overcome.

_____

1 mark

3 Suggest why all cars have oil put into their engines.

_____

_____

_____

2 marks

4 When Shelley Rudman won her Olympic medal in the bobsleigh skeleton, suggest **three** things she would have done to make sure she went as fast as possible.

1 mark

1 _____

1 mark

2 _____

1 mark

3 _____

Streamlining and air resistance

1 What happens to air resistance as you move faster?

_____

_____

2 a Why do dolphins have a streamlined shape?

_____

_____

_____

1 mark

b What are the **two** effects of increasing the streamlining of a car?

1 _____

2 _____

2 marks

3 a What happens to the air resistance when a skydiver opens their parachute?

_____

b Draw arrows on these four diagrams to show how the forces on a skydiver change as she falls to the ground.

A Just after she has jumped from the plane

B Just before she opens her parachute

C Just after she opens her parachute

D just before she reaches the ground.

4 What is the name given to the fastest speed that anything can travel at because air resistance has become as great as the forward force?

_____

mass

weight

1 If an apple has a mass of 100 g,
what is its weight?

_____

2 In which direction does gravitational force apply?

_____

3 Choose the correct numbers and units to complete the table about the
mass and weight of an astronaut.

50 kg	500 N	150 N	250 N	0 N	800 N	75 kg
1000 N	80 kg	15 kg	800 kg	900 kg	900 N	
90 kg	150 kg	15 N				

	On Earth	In deep space	On the Moon
Mass			90 kg
Weight			

5 marks

42

4 Jupiter is a much larger planet than the Earth.

a Suggest what would happen to the weight of an astronaut who travelled to Jupiter.

_____

1 mark

b Explain your answer.

_____

_____

_____

2 marks

5 Tick the box for the right combination of two factors that affect the size of the gravitational pull between two objects.

A Density and distance apart ☐

B Mass and weight ☐

C Mass and distance apart ☐

D Density and weight ☐

E Weight and speed of movement ☐

1 mark

6 a Which force did Galileo not take into account in his experiments on falling objects?

_____

1 mark

b Where was Galileo's experiment repeated and why could it be done properly there?

_____

_____

2 marks

1 Circle the right word or phrase from the choices in bold to complete these passages about the Earth, the Moon and the Sun.

The Moon orbits the Earth approximately once every **24 hours/7 days/ 28 days/365 days**. The Moon is a **luminous/non-luminous** object which we can see because it reflects the light from the Sun which is a **luminous/non-luminous** object.

The Earth orbits the Sun approximately once every **24 hours/7 days/ 28 days/365 days**. This length of time gives us our **day and night/ week/month/year**. The Earth is tilted on its axis so different parts of the Earth's surface face towards it at different times in its orbit around the Sun. This is what gives us **day and night/summer and winter**. The Earth also rotates on its own axis once every **24 hours/7 days/ 28 days/365 days** and this is what gives us **day and night/ summer and winter**.

8 marks

2 a Why does the amount of the Moon we can see from Earth vary at different times in the month?

_____

_____

_____

_____

2 marks

b Explain why the Sun and the Moon both look the same size from Earth.

_____

_____

_____

_____

2 marks

3 Complete this list showing the planets in our Solar System in order of their distance from the Sun, starting with the closest.

1 _____

2 Venus _____

3 _____

4 _____

5 _____

6 Saturn _____

7 _____

8 _____

9 _____

7 marks

4 a Complete the **four** statements by drawing lines to join the boxes.

The average distance from Venus to the Sun is...	150 million km
The average distance from Pluto to the Sun is...	0.38 million km
The average distance from Earth to the Moon is...	5900 million km
The average distance from Earth to the Sun is...	108 million km

4 marks

b Which of these is a star?

The Moon ☐

The Earth ☐

The Sun ☐

Mars ☐

1 mark

1

How could this apparatus be used to tell if a piece of iron was itself a magnet?

_____

_____

2 marks

2

Draw the magnetic field you would expect to see around this magnet.

2 marks

3 What is the difference between an ordinary magnet like this and an electromagnet?

_____

_____

1 mark

4 What element is used to make the core of an electromagnet?

_____

1 mark

5 Look carefully at this diagram.

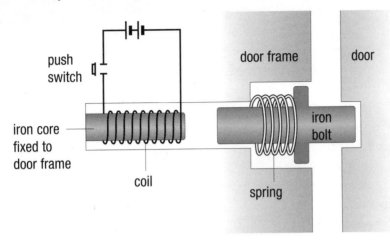

push switch

door frame

door

iron core fixed to door frame

iron bolt

coil

spring

a When the switch is pushed, the iron bolt moves to the left and the door opens. Explain why this happens.

_____

_____

_____

_____

2 marks

b When the switch is released, what will the iron bolt do?

_____

_____

1 mark

c Would this door lock work if the bolt was made of aluminium?

_____

1 mark

d Explain your answer.

_____

_____

_____

2 marks

Solids, liquids and gases

1 Complete the table below.

Description	State of matter	Particle diagram
The particles are in a fixed lattice pattern and although they vibrate they do not have enough energy to move away from each other.		
The particles have lots of energy and spread out to fill all the available space.		
The particles are in contact with each other but can move and slide over each other.		

6 marks

2 a Complete the table below to say which of the substances would be a gas, solid or a liquid at normal room temperature.

Substance	Melting point (°C)	Boiling point (°C)	Solid, liquid or gas
A	0	100	
B	−183	−162	
C	100	245	
D	−39	355	
E	1540	Above 2000	

5 marks

b Which of these do you know is water?

_____

1 mark

c Which do you think might be iron?

_____

1 mark

3 a What happens to any substance when it gets hotter?

_____

1 mark

b Explain your answer by describing what happens to the particles.

_____

_____

_____

3 marks

4

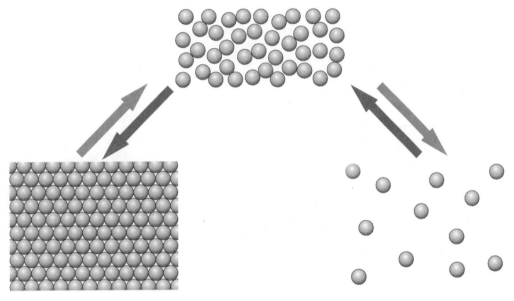

4 marks

Write the correct name of each change of state next to each arrow.

5 If you spray a small amount of perfume into a room, the people close to it will smell it straight away and, after a time, people at the other side of the room will be able to smell it too.

Explain why this happens by describing how the particles in a gas behave.

_____

_____

_____

2 marks

1 If you added 25 g of salt to 125 g of water, what mass of solution would you have?

_____

2 marks

2 Some students had a mixture of sand, salt and iron filings which they wanted to separate.

   a Put these statements in order to show the sequence they followed to do this.

      A Filter the mixture of sand, salt and water to separate the sand from the salt water solution.

      B Add water to the sand and salt.

      C Use a magnet to extract the iron filings.

      D Heat the salt water solution so that the water evaporates leaving the salt behind.

      _____

4 marks

   b List the apparatus you would need to use for each stage.

      _____

      _____

      _____

      _____

4 marks

3 Match words from the box below to the definitions.

solute	solution	solvent	insoluble

   a Formed when a solid dissolves in a liquid.   _____

1 mark

   b The solid that dissolves in a liquid.   _____

1 mark

   c The liquid that a solid dissolves in.   _____

1 mark

   d When a solid will not dissolve in a particular liquid.   _____

1 mark

4 Look at the diagrams below of different methods of separating substances.

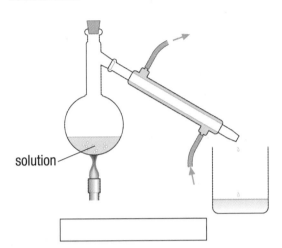

solution

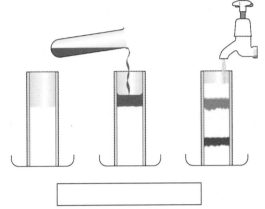

solution

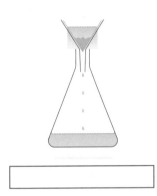

a Choose from the following words to label each separation technique with its correct name.

| chromatography distillation evaporation filtration |

4 marks

b Match the correctly named separation technique to the mixture that it could be used for.

i Separating the different coloured food dyes that make up the colour of a purple Smartie. _____

1 mark

ii The water from the dye in black ink. _____

1 mark

iii To get a solution of dissolved coffee in water from large pieces of ground coffee beans. _____

1 mark

iv To get blue copper sulphate crystals from a solution of copper sulphate in water. _____

1 mark

PARTICLES — Elements, compounds and mixtures

1 a Complete the table to show which of these substances are elements, compounds and mixtures.

Substance	Element, compound or mixture
Oxygen	
Air	
Steel	
Iron	
Water	

5 marks

b Explain the difference between a compound and a mixture.

_____

_____

_____

1 mark

2 Put the correct symbol next to the name of the element it represents.

P	S	Na	K	H	O	C	Cu	Ni	N

Element	Symbol	Element	Symbol
Hydrogen		Phosphorus	
Nitrogen		Sulphur	
Sodium		Potassium	
Oxygen		Carbon	
Copper		Nickel	

10 marks

3 Look at the chemical formulae for these compounds and decide which elements have reacted together to produce them.

CO_2 _____ and _____

H_2O _____ and _____

NH_3 _____ and _____

NaCl _____ and _____

CuO _____ and _____

5 marks

4 Which of these statements about chemical and physical changes are true and which are false?

a In a chemical change new substances are formed.

TRUE/FALSE

b In physical changes new substances are formed.

TRUE/FALSE

c Chemical changes are easy to reverse.

TRUE/FALSE

d Physical changes are easy to reverse.

TRUE/FALSE

4 marks

5 a What is the common name for sodium chloride?

1 mark

_____

b Describe the two elements that react to make sodium chloride.

1 mark

i Sodium is _____

1 mark

ii Chlorine is _____

1 a Which is easier to reverse – a chemical change or a physical change?

_____

1 mark

b Give an example of a physical change of state.

_____

1 mark

c Give an example of a chemical reaction.

_____

1 mark

2 a What is the proper name for burning a substance in oxygen?

_____

1 mark

b What compound is formed when iron reacts with oxygen?

_____

1 mark

c What name do we usually give this compound?

_____

1 mark

3 Choose the correct words from the box to make up the word equations given below. You may need to use some words more than once.

water	oxygen	magnesium oxide	carbon dioxide
sodium	chlorine	magnesium	glucose	sodium chloride

a The formation of common salt.

_____ + _____ → _____

1 mark

b The oxidation of magnesium.

_____ + _____ → _____

1 mark

c Photosynthesis.

_____

_____ + _____ → _____ + _____

_____

1 mark

4 What is the proper name for a chemical reaction that takes in heat?

_____

5

The same chemical reaction is happening in both these pictures.
What element is needed to make this reaction happen?

_____

1 mark

6 Respiration is a chemical reaction.

   a What are the reactants?

_____

_____

1 mark

   b What are the products?

_____

_____

1 mark

levels
4-6

1 What do we call a reaction where an acid is mixed with an alkali to form a substance with a pH of around 7?

_____

1 mark

2 This is the pH scale.

1	2	3	4	5	6	7	8	9	10	11	12	13	14

Mark on this diagram where you would expect to find:

a lemon juice

b water

c hair shampoo

3 marks

3 a When an acid reacts with an alkali a certain type of compound is produced.

Complete the word equation for this type of reaction:

Acid + alkali → _____ + _____

 2 marks

b Complete the word equation for the reaction between hydrochloric acid and sodium hydroxide.

Hydrochloric acid + sodium hydroxide → _____ + _____

 2 marks

c Complete the word equation for this reaction:

Acid + metal → _____ + _____

 2 marks

d Describe the test for the gas given off in this reaction.

_____

_____

1 mark

e What kind of salt is always formed in reactions with nitric acid?

_____

1 mark

f Complete the word equation for this reaction:

Nitric acid + calcium hydroxide → _____ + _____

 2 marks

4 Sulphur dioxide is released into the air when fossil fuels are burned. What affect can this have on the environment?

_____

1 mark

5 Circle the correct answer to show which of these would turn litmus paper blue and which would make it red.

Substance	Colour of litmus
Lemon juice	Red / blue
Toothpaste	Red / blue
Vinegar	Red / blue
Cola	Red / blue
Soap	Red / blue
Bleach	Red / blue

6 marks

6 Bee stings are acidic and wasp stings are alkaline. Suggest which of the substances in question 5 could be used to treat:

a A bee sting

_____

1 mark

b A wasp sting

_____

1 mark

c Explain how you made your choices.

_____

_____

_____

3 marks

1 Decide which of these statements are properties of metals and which are properties of non-metals.

A Good conductors of heat

B Poor conductors of electricity

C Generally solids at room temperature

D Solids, liquids and gases at room temperature

E Shiny appearance

Add the letters in the correct column to complete the table below.

Properties of metals	Properties of non-metals

5 marks

2 a What needs to be present for the production of iron oxide?

1 _____

2 _____

3 _____

3 marks

b What name do we usually give to iron oxide?

_____

1 mark

c Suggest **one** way in which iron surfaces can be protected from the formation of iron oxide.

_____

1 mark

3 Look at this table and decide which metal could be copper and which could be gold. Give your reasons.

Metal	Reacts with cold water	Reacts with dilute acid	Reacts with oxygen	Appearance
A	Yes	Yes	Yes	Silver grey
B	No	No	No	Yellow
C	No	Yes	Yes	Dark grey
D	No	Yes (slowly)	Yes	Yellow
E	Yes (slowly)	Yes	Yes	Grey

a Metal _____ is copper because _____

_____

b Metal _____ is gold because _____

_____

4 Place these metals in order of reactivity.

copper	zinc	potassium	lead	mercury

Most reactive _____

_____

_____

_____

Least reactive _____

Rocks and the rock cycle

1 Name the **three** main groups of rock.

1 _____

2 _____

3 _____

3 marks

2 Complete the diagram by labelling the types of rock.

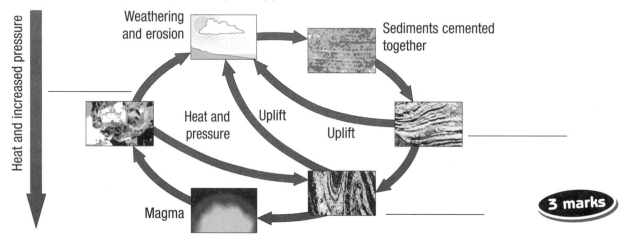

Heat and increased pressure

Weathering and erosion

Sediments cemented together

Heat and pressure   Uplift   Uplift

Magma

3 marks

3 Match the statement about rock structure to the explanation about how they are formed.

Sedimentary rocks contain fossils	Rocks that form when molten rock from volcanoes cool slowly have larger crystals than when the cooling process is very quick.
Granite is an igneous rock with large crystals	When sedimentary rocks are heated under pressure the resulting rock is much harder.
Limestone is a soft rock that crumbles easily	The remains of dead sea creatures fall to the sea bed with the sediment from rocks and get trapped between the layers.
Marble is a hard metamorphic rock	Rocks that form when layers of sediment build up on the sea bed are usually soft.

4 marks

4 a What does the word 'metamorphic' mean?

1 mark

_____

b What type of metamorphic rock is formed from sandstone?

1 mark

_____

c How are metamorphic rocks such as marble different from sedimentary rocks such as limestone?

1 mark

_____

5 Describe what is happening in each of these pictures.

a

_____

_____

_____

b

_____

_____

_____

c

_____

_____

3 marks

_____

Food chains and food webs

1 Put these organisms into the right order for a food chain.

A Secondary consumer

B Producer

C Primary consumer

D Tertiary consumer

2 Circle the correct word or phrase from the choices in bold to complete the passage.

Food chains and food webs always have a green plant at the beginning. This is because **all animals need to eat vegetables/green plants grow everywhere/only green plants can make their own food**. The first animal in a food chain is called **a producer/a primary consumer/a secondary consumer**. This animal is always **a herbivore/a carnivore/an omnivore**. The animals that eat the plants are then often eaten by other animals. The animal that is eaten is called **prey/a predator** and the animal that eats the other creature is called **prey/a predator**. In the food chain the predator is known as the **producer/primary consumer/secondary consumer**.

3 What does the arrow in a food chain show?

4

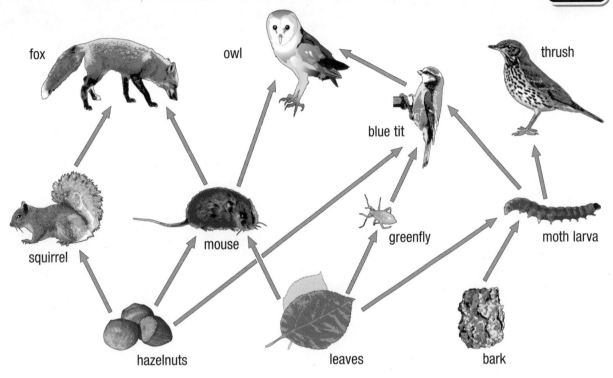

fox owl thrush blue tit squirrel mouse greenfly moth larva hazelnuts leaves bark

a Write **two** food chains that the owl is part of.

_____

_____

2 marks

b Draw a pyramid of numbers for **one** of the food chains you have chosen.

3 marks

Energy transfers in food chains and food webs

1 a What **three** main functions do living things use energy for?

_____

_____

_____

b Which of these represents the energy that can be passed up the food chain?

_____

1 mark

2

100% energy from food

5% other life processes

10% movement energy

10% lost in excretions

Energy for growth

70% lost to surroundings as heat

a Calculate the amount of energy the squirrel has left for growth.

_____

_____

b Draw a pie chart to represent how the energy the squirrel takes in from its food is distributed.

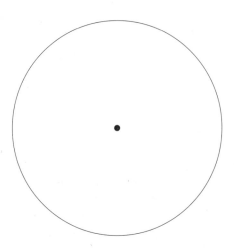

3 Which of these statements are true and which are false?

a Most of the energy that an animal eats is lost to its surroundings as heat.

TRUE/FALSE

b Food chains are never more than three or four organisms long because most creatures are very fussy about what they eat.

TRUE/FALSE

c Food chains are only three or four organisms long because of the amount of energy lost at each stage.

TRUE/FALSE

d About 10% of the energy an animal takes in as food is transferred to movement energy.

TRUE/FALSE

e About 50% of the energy that an animal takes in as food is transferred to the next creature in the food chain.

TRUE/FALSE

5 marks

Variation and inheritance

1 Jane and Sarah are identical twins: they both have blue eyes; Sarah has blond hair but Jane has red hair.

   a What do you think one of the twins has done to change her appearance?

   _____

1 mark

   b Explain your answer.

   _____

   _____

   _____

2 marks

2 Robert and Matthew are brothers. Robert has red hair and Matthew has dark brown hair.

   a Does this mean that one boy has changed his natural hair colour?

   _____

1 mark

   b Explain your answer.

   _____

   _____

   _____

2 marks

3 The Jones family has five sons. They all have dark brown hair and three of them have blue eyes and two have brown eyes. Three of them can play the piano and two are very good swimmers.

Which of these characteristics are inherited from their parents and which are environmental characteristics?

Environmental	Inherited

4 marks

4 A plant breeder is very keen to have plants with blue flowers as they sell the best. He takes 10 cuttings from each of six plants and this is what happens when the cuttings grow and flower.

Plant cuttings are taken from	Red flowering plants	Blue flowering plants
A	5	5
B	6	4
C	10	0
D	9	1
E	0	10
F	2	8

Blue flowers sell so well that he needs to take cuttings from at least three plants to make sure he has got enough.

a Which **three** should he choose?

_____

_____

_____

3 marks

All his original plants are affected by a disease except plants A and B, which seem to be able to resist the disease.

b Which plant should he continue to take cuttings from?

_____

1 mark

c Explain your answer.

_____

_____

_____

3 marks

1 Choose **two** characteristics that help polar bears to live in their habitat.

   A A good sense of smell.

   B Thick fur to trap heat and keep it warm.

   C Sharp claws to help grip on icy surfaces.

   D Small ears as it is quite quiet on the polar ice.

   E Blue eyes to contrast with its white coat.

   _____

2 marks

2 a Look at the adaptations in the box below.

migration of birds   **hibernation**
deciduous trees   **nocturnal hunting**

   Decide which are daily adaptations and which are seasonal adaptations to complete the table.

Daily adaptations	Seasonal adaptations

4 marks

b Explain why some animals hibernate.

   _____

   _____

   _____

2 marks

c What does nocturnal mean?

   _____

1 mark

d Some birds fly hundreds of miles to spend part of the year in one place and then rest in another. Suggest a reason why they do this.

   _____

   _____

2 marks

3 From this list of plant adaptations, choose **three** factors that enable cacti to grow in hot dry desert conditions.

    A Flowers that open in the day and close at night.

    B Swollen stems to store water.

    C Flowers that trap insects.

    D Small spines for leaves.

    E Long roots to find water below ground.

    F Losing their leaves in winter.

_____

3 marks

4 Imagine a habitat where:

it is very hot and wet in summer

it is very cold and wet in winter

there are a lot of trees that grow very lush in the summer but are all deciduous so have no leaves at all in winter

the ground is always wet and muddy

there are a lot of species of insect including those who feed on the blood of other creatures.

    a Choose **one** adaptation that you think would be important for an ANIMAL living in this habitat and say why you have chosen it.

_____

_____

_____

1 mark

    b Choose **one** adaptation you think would be important for a PLANT living in this habitat and again say why this would be important.

_____

_____

_____

1 mark

1 a What name is given to the group of animals that all have backbones?

_____

1 mark

   b This group of animals is further divided into **five** smaller groups –
what are they?

1 _____

2 _____

3 _____

4 _____

5 _____

5 marks

2 Which group of vertebrates does each of these characteristics apply to?

   a Can live both on land and under water.   _____

   b Have feathers.   _____

   c Breathe through gills.   _____

   d Feed their young on milk from the mother.   _____

   e Have dry scaly skins.   _____

5 marks

3 Which group of **invertebrates** have three-sectioned bodies and three
pairs of legs?

_____

1 mark

4 A new species has recently been found in the rainforests of Borneo. It
has a small body about the size of a saucer with two parts to it and four
pairs of legs. It does not have a backbone.

Which group of invertebrates does it belong to?

_____

1 mark

5 The four main groups of Arthropods – the biggest group of invertebrates – are:

Insects

Arachnids

Crustaceans

Myriapods

Put the arthropods from the box into the right group in the table below.

| grasshopper | spider | lobster | millipede |
| wasp | scorpion | crab | dragonfly |

Insect	Arachnid	Crustacean	Myriapod

8 marks

Using keys to identify living things

1 In a new supermarket the Manager is trying to decide where to put certain items. He draws up this key to help him.

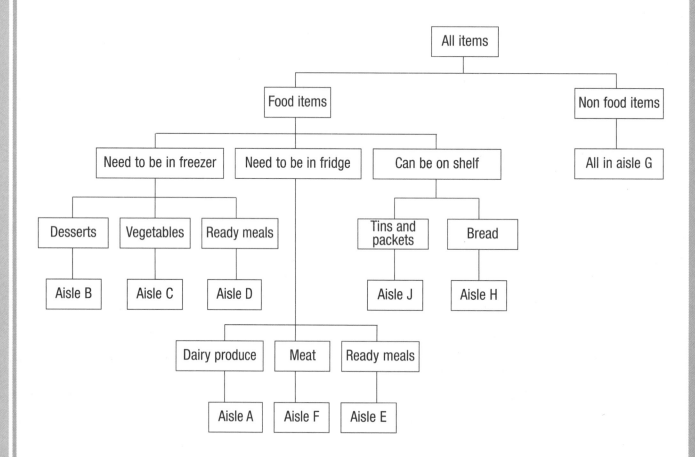

Using this key, decide which aisle these items should go in:

a Frozen peas _____

b Birthday cards _____

c A loaf of brown bread _____

d Chilled pizza _____

e Cheese _____

5 marks

2

Horse

Walks on four legs, has hooves

Dog

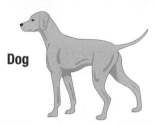

Walks on four legs, gives birth to a number of young at once

Human

Walks on two legs

Owl

Has feathers, lays eggs

Dolphin

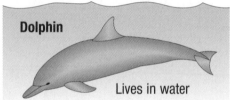

Lives in water

Imagine you are an alien from outer space – you have just arrived on Earth and you want to know which species of animal is which.

Complete this key to help the alien identify these Earth creatures. The first question has been done for you. You should need to write **three** more questions.

Q1 Does the creature have feathers?
If YES, it is an owl.
If NO, go to question 2.

Q2 _____
If _____ , it is a _____
If _____ , go to question 3.

Q3 _____
If _____ , it is a _____
If _____ , go to question 4.

Q4 _____
If _____ , it is a _____
If _____ , it is a _____

3 marks

Competition among living things

levels
4-6

1 What is meant when a species of plant or animal is said to be extinct?

_____

_____

_____

1 mark

2 Explain why is there often a patch of bare earth under a large tree or shrub?

_____

_____

_____

1 mark

3 Suggest why woodland plants often flower in early spring rather than later in the year when there is more sunlight.

_____

_____

_____

2 marks

4 Foxes eat rabbits. If there is an outbreak of disease among rabbits and many die, explain what will happen to the fox population.

_____

_____

_____

2 marks

5 Many small flowering plants grow under the trees in woodlands.
A number of trees are blown down.

To explain what will happen to the numbers of the small flowering plants
and why, decide which of these statements are true and which are false.

a The numbers will stay the same because they are not affected by the trees.   **TRUE/FALSE**

b The numbers will go up because there is more light so the plants will
grow more.   **TRUE/FALSE**

c The numbers will go down because they will no longer have the
protection of the trees.   **TRUE/FALSE**

d The numbers will go up because there will be more room so more seeds
will germinate.   **TRUE/FALSE**

6 Look at the graph showing how the population of rabbits in a wood
changed over time.

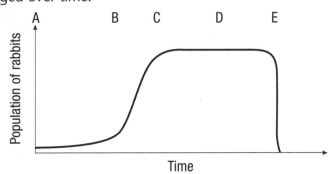

a What happened to the population of rabbits in the period from
C to D?

_____

b What time of year do you think might be represented by B?

_____

c What happens to the population at D?

_____

d Can you suggest what might have caused this?

4 marks

_____

1 Tick the boxes to show which of these environmental problems can be caused by burning fossil fuels.

The damage to the ozone layer ☐

The greenhouse effect ☐

The cutting down of forests to create space to grow crops ☐

Global warming ☐

Acid rain ☐

2 marks

2 a What can be done to improve the habitat in a lake that has been affected by acid rain?

_____

_____

_____

1 mark

b What kind of chemical reaction is involved?

_____

1 mark

3 Describe the environmental damage done by the chemicals called CFCs.

_____

_____

_____

2 marks

4 What illness in humans may be increasing because of damage to the ozone layer?

_____

1 mark

5 Circle the correct word or phrase from the choices in bold to complete
the passage.

Chemicals that are used to kill pests are called **pesticides/herbicides**.

An example is slug pellets which are used to kill slugs. Slugs in turn are

eaten by **prey/predators** such as thrushes which are **prey/predators**

of bigger birds such as sparrowhawks. The thrushes will eat a lot of

slugs and so the pesticide will **spread out/build up** in their bodies.

This might not be enough to kill the thrushes, but when a sparrowhawk

eats a number of thrushes, the pesticide will **spread out/build up**

in the body of the sparrowhawk and kill it.

5 marks

6 Describe how an increase in the human population of the Earth can
affect other species of plants and animals.

_____

_____

_____

_____

_____

_____

2 marks

Asking questions and making predictions

1 For **each** of these investigations, write a clear question.

a To investigate candles burning in air.

Question _____

_____

_____

b To investigate where woodlice like to live.

Question _____

_____

_____

c To investigate the speed of different sized falling objects.

Question _____

_____

_____

d To investigate the friction of different surfaces.

Question _____

_____

_____

e To investigate energy in food.

Question _____

_____

_____

2 Make a prediction using your scientific knowledge for each of the
questions on the previous page.

a I think that _____

_____

Because _____

_____

_____

b I think that _____

_____

Because _____

_____

_____

c I think that _____

_____

Because _____

_____

_____

d I think that _____

_____

Because _____

_____

_____

e I think that _____

_____

Because _____

_____

1 For **three** of the investigations you thought about on the last page, decide what will be your independent variable, your dependent variable and what you will keep the same to make it a fair test.

a Question _____

Independent variable _____

Dependent variable _____

To make sure it is a fair test _____

_____

3 marks

b Question _____

Independent variable _____

Dependent variable _____

To make sure it is a fair test _____

_____

3 marks

c Question _____

Independent variable _____

Dependent variable _____

To make sure it is a fair test _____

_____

3 marks

2 Which of the variables below are continuous and which are discontinuous?

a The thickness of the trunks of trees in a woodland.

CONTINUOUS/DISCONTINUOUS

1 mark

b The electric current flowing in a circuit.

CONTINUOUS/DISCONTINUOUS

1 mark

c The number of boys and the number of girls in each year group in a school.

CONTINUOUS/DISCONTINUOUS

1 mark

3 Circle the correct word or phrase from the choices in bold to complete this paragraph about some pupils carrying out an investigation.

When you want to carry out a scientific investigation you first need to decide on a question which enables you to see clearly what you are trying to find out. This will help you to choose the correct variables. The thing you are going to change is called the **dependent/independent/control** variable. The thing you measure is called the **dependent/independent/control** variable. To make your investigation a fair test you must **alter as many things as possible/only alter one variable**. The things you keep the same are called **dependent/independent/control** variables. You should **have as many of these as possible/only control one variable**. When you have taken your results, it is a good idea to display them in a chart or graph. This is because **it looks nice/it makes it easy to see trends in your results**. If your independent variable was discontinuous then you should draw a **bar chart/line graph**. If your independent variable was continuous you should draw a **bar chart/line of best fit**. Your independent variable should go along the *x-axis/y-axis* of your graph.

4 In some experiments it can be very difficult to control all the factors other than the one you want to test. Suggest what kind of factors might be especially hard to control.

_____

_____

_____

1 mark

1 Some pupils carried out an experiment to see if the temperature of water affected the amount of salt which would dissolve.

a What would be their independent variable?

_____

1 mark

b What would be their dependent variable?

_____

1 mark

c What factors should they keep the same?

1 _____

2 _____

3 _____

3 marks

d In the box below, draw a results table for them to put their findings into.

2 marks

e What sort of graph or chart should they use to display these results?

1 mark

_____

f Explain your answer.

_____

_____

2 marks

g Some pupils carried out this experiment and this is what they recorded.

We weighed out some salt and tried to dissolve it in water at different temperatures to see how much would dissolve. Different people tried different temperatures but we all used salt from the same packet and 150 ml beakers of water to keep it a fair test. We found that at 50 °C 3.9 g dissolved, at 80 °C it was 6 g, at 30 °C it was 1.7 g, at 70 °C it was 4.7 g, at 40 °C, 1.9 g and at 60 °C, 3.3 g.

Put their results into your table on page 82.

2 marks

h On the graph paper below display these results in the best possible way.

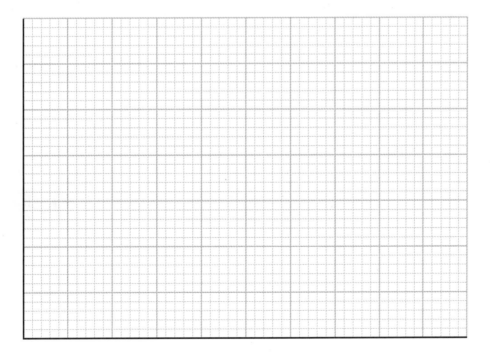

8 marks

Patterns and relationships

levels
4-5

1 Some pupils did an experiment to see if water evaporated more quickly in different conditions. They put some beakers of water in different places around the school and some outside.

Tom recorded the results for his group in his exercise book. They looked like this:

On the windowsill 145 ml after 3 days, on the teacher's desk 150 ml, on outside windowsill all water gone.

Peter's group recorded their results like this:

Location and temperature at start	Start volume (ml)	Volume after 1 day (ml)	Volume after 2 days (ml)	Volume after 3 days (ml)
Classroom windowsill (28 °C)	150	142	136	131
Teacher's desk (23 °C)	150	146	142	138
In corner of corridor (19 °C)	150	148	146	144
Outside windowsill (15 °C)	150	143	135	130

a Which set of results are better: Tom's or Peter's?

_____

1 mark

b Explain why.

_____

_____

_____

2 marks

c Can you see a pattern in Tom's results?

_____

1 mark

d Describe the relationship between temperature at the start and rate of evaporation in Peter's results.

_____

_____

2 marks

e Which line in Peter's results table spoils this pattern?

_____

1 mark

f Can you suggest an explanation for this?

_____

_____

1 mark

g What can you see in Peter's results to show that they tried to make it a fair test?

_____

1 mark

Before they collected their results, Tom's group wrote a prediction like this:

We think that the shape of the container will affect how quickly the water evaporates and the containers with a wide top will make the water evaporate faster than containers with a narrow top.

h Explain whether or not you think this is a good prediction.

_____

_____

_____

1 mark

i Can they say from their results whether the prediction was right or wrong?

_____

1 mark

j Describe an experiment they could do to test this prediction.

_____

_____

_____

_____

_____

_____

3 marks

k What pattern would they have been looking for in their results?

_____

1 mark

1

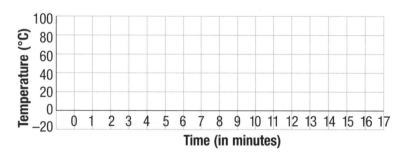

Look at the graph of temperature against time.

a After how long had all the ice melted?

1 mark

_____

b How long did it take for the water to reach 40 °C?

1 mark

_____

c At what time do you think someone observing this experiment would have started to notice bubbles in the water?

1 mark

_____

The same water was then left to cool and the temperature again taken every minute.

d On the axes below sketch the shape that you think this graph would have.

3 marks

e Explain your answer.

_____

_____

_____

3 marks

levels
4-5

2 Look at the bar chart.

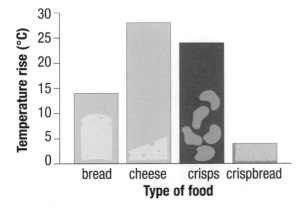

a From this chart put the foodstuffs in order from the one with the highest energy content to the one with the lowest.

Highest energy _____

_____

_____

Lowest energy _____

b Explain how you made your choices.

_____

_____

_____

c Why have the results of this experiment been displayed in a bar chart and not a line graph?

_____

_____

levels
5-6

1 Write down **three** sources of evidence you could make use of if you wanted to test an idea.

_____

_____

_____

3 marks

2 In an experiment to see if bean shoots grew faster in warmer conditions, some pupils found these results after 10 days.

Temperature (°C)	Height of bean shoot (cm)
5	0
10	2
15	5
20	9
25	2
30	2
40	0

The pupils displayed their results in a graph.

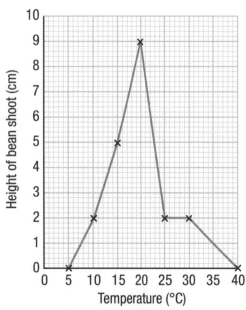

a   **i**   Is this evidence to show that bean shoots grow faster in warmer conditions?   **YES/NO**

     ii   Explain your answer.

_____

_____

_____

b   **i**   Is this evidence to show that there is an ideal temperature at which to grow bean shoots?   **YES/NO**

     ii   Explain your answer.

_____

_____

_____

c   **i**   Is this evidence to show that bean shoots grow better if they get plenty of water?   **YES/NO**

     ii   Explain your answer.

_____

_____

_____

d   **i**   On the graph on page 88, is this a line of best fit?   **YES/NO**

     ii   Explain your answer.

_____

_____

_____

3   We now know that the Earth goes around the Sun, but in the past people thought it was the other way and that the Sun went round the Earth.

Suggest why you think scientific ideas change over time.

_____

_____

_____

1 If you were going to repeat the bean growing experiment on the last page, can you suggest **two** things that would make it better?

1 _____

2 _____

2 marks

2 Which of these experiments do you think were fair tests?

a A group of pupils increased the number of cells connected to an electrical circuit and read the current from an ammeter each time to see if the number of cells increased the current flowing in the circuit. **FAIR TEST/NOT FAIR TEST**

b Another group of pupils did the same experiment but this time they added more bulbs each time they increased the number of cells. Again they took readings from an ammeter to see if increasing the number of cells increased the current in the circuit. **FAIR TEST/NOT FAIR TEST**

c A class were testing a variety of shoes for friction by measuring the force needed to move them on different surfaces. Some of the surfaces were outside and the experiment was done over two lessons. On the day of the second lesson it rained. **FAIR TEST/NOT FAIR TEST**

3 marks

3 A group of pupils wanted to test the effect of fizzy drinks on pulse rate. They all drank some of their favourite fizzy drink and then measured their pulse rates.

a List **three** things that would have made this a better experiment.

1 _____

2 _____

3 _____

3 marks

b Suggest why this might not have been a fair test even if they had done all of these things.

_____

_____

_____

1 mark

4 A farmer had had a problem for several years with a particular insect attacking his crop of maize. He decided to carry out an experiment. In one field he planted the same kind of maize but sprayed it regularly with a pesticide designed to kill this sort of insect. In another field he planted a new type of maize that is meant to be resistant to this insect.

What questions would he need to ask at the end of the year to see which, if either, of these had been successful?

_____

_____

_____

3 marks

5 When new medicines are being tested, a group of people are given the new medicine and another group are not. Choose one of the following statements to explain why no-one ever knows which group they are in.

A New medicines are always very expensive.

B The people who are not given the new medicine are a control group to see if what happens to the others is really because of the new medicine.

C If the new medicine doesn't work properly then you have only harmed half as many people.

1 mark

_____

1 a Which of these sources of energy are renewable and which are non-renewable?

Draw a line from each energy source to the correct box.

Energy source

wind power	
coal	RENEWABLE
solar power	
biomass	
natural gas	NON-RENEWABLE
oil	

3 marks

b Where did the energy that is stored in all of these sources come from?

_____

1 mark

2

Oak tree leaf

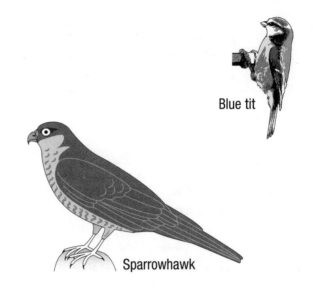

Sparrowhawk

Blue tit

Caterpillar

a Arrange these living things into a food chain below.

☐ 2 marks

b Explain how you chose the first thing in your food chain.

_____

_____

_____

☐ 1 mark

c Which **three** structures do plant cells have that animal cells do not?

1 _____

2 _____

3 _____

☐ 3 marks

d Which **one** of these do plants need to make their own food?

_____

☐ 1 mark

Total

maximum 11 marks ☐

93

3 The pH scale is used to measure how acidic or alkaline a substance is.

1	2	3	4	5	6	7	8	9	10	11	12	13	14

a Mark on the scale where you would expect to find an acid.

b In the box below, put the pH number you would expect for each of these substances.

Substance	pH
Lemon juice	
Water	
Sodium hydroxide	

4

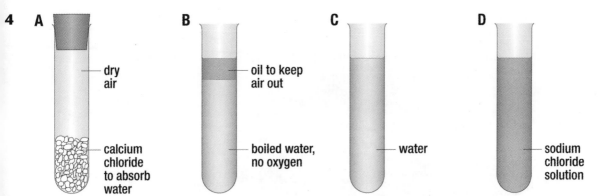

A — dry air
— calcium chloride to absorb water

B — oil to keep air out
— boiled water, no oxygen

C — water

D — sodium chloride solution

Some students set up an experiment to see what made iron nails go rusty. They put a nail into each of the test tubes and left them for a week. At the end of the week they examined the nails.

a Give the letter of the test tube that you would expect to contain the nail with the most rust?

_____

1 mark

b Two nails will not rust at all. Give the letters of the test tubes containing these nails.

_____ and _____

1 mark

c If instead of iron nails, the students had put gold rings into the test tubes and left them for a week – what would they have seen?

_____

_____

_____

1 mark

Total

maximum 8 marks

5

The boat is floating on the water.

a Draw **two** arrows on the diagram to show the forces and label them.

b What can you say about the forces acting on the boat?

_____

_____

_____

6 A breeder of pedigree dogs wants as many puppies as possible who are single colour rather than black and white. He looked at the puppies from his most recent litters.

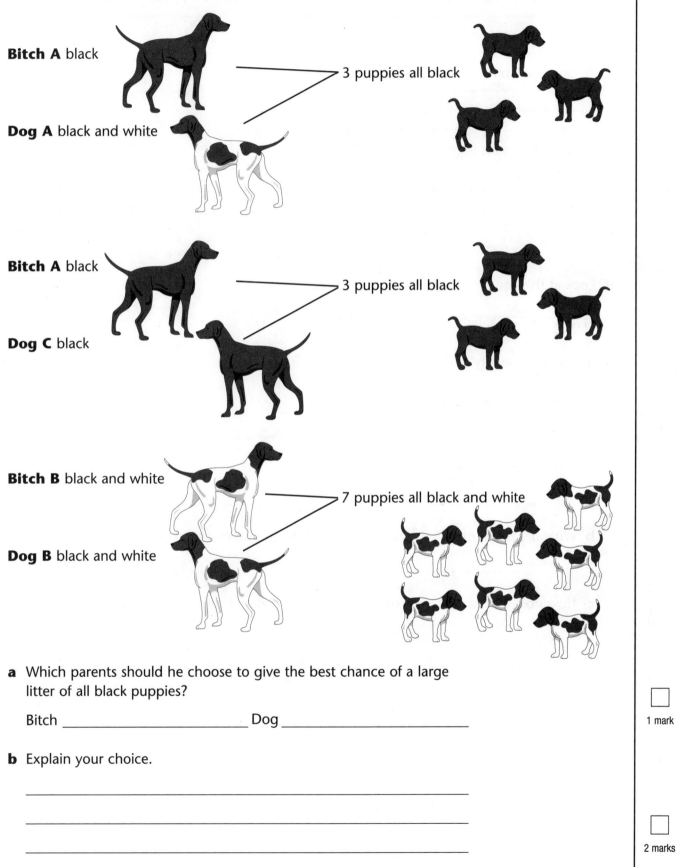

Bitch A black

Dog A black and white

3 puppies all black

Bitch A black

Dog C black

3 puppies all black

Bitch B black and white

Dog B black and white

7 puppies all black and white

a Which parents should he choose to give the best chance of a large litter of all black puppies?

Bitch _____ Dog _____

1 mark

b Explain your choice.

_____

_____

_____

2 marks

Total

maximum 6 marks

7 Choose a separating technique from the box for each mixture in the table.

chromatography	distillation	evaporation	filtration

To get sand from a mixture of sand and water	
To get water from black ink	
To get salt crystals from sea water	
To find how many food dyes are in a blue Smartie	

4 marks

8 Look at this equation for a chemical reaction:

$$2Na + Cl_2 \rightarrow 2NaCl$$

a Can you identify the compound that is made here:

   i by its proper name?

   _____

1 mark

   ii by its everyday name?

   _____

1 mark

b What are the names of the **two** elements that go into this reaction?

_____ and _____

2 marks

c How do we know that a chemical reaction has taken place?

_____

1 mark

9 Scientists need to collect evidence to help them develop their ideas. Evidence can come from a lot of different sources.

a In the list below, tick the boxes that you think would be sources of evidence.

Source of information	Evidence
An experiment you carried out at school.	☐
What your Granny thinks.	☐
What your teacher thinks.	☐
The results of a survey published in a scientific journal.	☐
A TV interview with a famous scientist about an experiment she has been doing.	☐
Something written in your science textbook.	☐

☐ 3 marks

To gather evidence it is sometimes necessary to carry out an experiment. All experiments need a factor to change (the independent variable) and a factor to observe or measure (the dependent variable).

b For each of the enquiries below, decide what would be a suitable independent and dependent variable.

    i Do plants grow better in bright light?

    Independent variable _____

    Dependent variable   _____

☐ 2 marks

    ii What material is best for insulating cups of hot drinks?

    Independent variable _____

    Dependent variable   _____

☐ 2 marks

    iii Does the amount of water affect the growth of bean plants?

    Independent variable _____

    Dependent variable _____

☐ 2 marks

Total

maximum 18 marks ☐

10 This information was given on the labels of some foods bought in a supermarket.

Per 100 g	Food A	Food B	Food C
Energy	477 kcal	141 kcal	340 kcal
Protein	4.5 g	3.5 g	10.1 g
Fat	18.3 g	7.0 g	22.6 g
Carbohydrate	73.6 g	16.1 g	25.2 g

a Why is the information given 'Per 100 g'?

_____

_____

2 marks

b Which food has the highest energy content?

_____

1 mark

c If you were given samples of foods A, B and C, how could you test them to find out which was which? Describe below an experiment you could carry out.

_____

_____

_____

_____

_____

_____

_____

_____

_____

_____

_____

_____

_____

3 marks

11 When fossil fuels are burned some gases are released into the atmosphere.
One of the gases causes acid rain.

a What is the name of this gas?

_____

1 mark

b Explain how this gas produces acid rain.

_____

_____

_____

2 marks

c What can happen when this rain falls onto lakes and rivers?

_____

_____

_____

2 marks

d What can be done to correct this?

_____

_____

_____

1 mark

e What is the name of the chemical reaction that takes place?

_____

1 mark

Total

maximum 13 marks

12

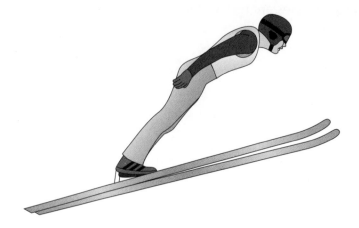

Look at the picture of the ski jumper.

a Describe **two** factors she has used to increase her maximum possible speed through the air.

1 _____

2 _____

b What is the correct name for the maximum speed she can achieve?

_____

c The car in the picture below is not travelling at its maximum speed, its speed is still increasing.

Draw arrows on the diagram to show the forces acting on the car.

2 marks

d   **i** In the course of a journey the car travels 100 miles in 4 hours. What is its average speed?

_____

_____

_____

_____

_____

2 marks

   ii Does this mean that the car has travelled at the same speed for the whole 100 miles?

_____

1 mark

   iii Explain your answer.

_____

_____

_____

_____

2 marks

Total

maximum 10 marks

13 Some pupils did an experiment to see if jelly dissolved more quickly in hotter water. This table shows their results.

Temperature (°C)	Time for jelly to dissolve (minutes)
30	12.6
40	10.9
50	9.2
60	9.1
70	5.8
80	4.1

a Name **two** factors or variables that they should have kept the same in order to make sure their experiment was a fair test.

_____

_____

2 marks

b **i** Use the results to plot a graph.
Label the axes and draw a line of best fit through the points.

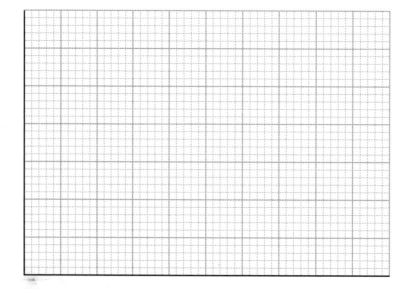

5 marks

1 mark

ii There is one result which seems to be anomalous (wrong).
Draw a circle around this point on your graph.

c One of the pupils wrote this in their exercise book as a conclusion:

> The temperature of the water did affect how quickly the jelly dissolved.

Another pupil said this was not a very scientific conclusion.

   i Why do you think this conclusion is not very scientific?

_____

_____

_____

   ii Write a better conclusion for this experiment.

_____

_____

_____

14

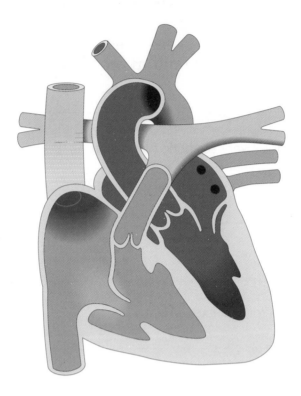

a **i** In which of the systems of the human body is this the major organ?

_____

ii The blood in the left-hand side of the heart has come from the lungs. Which gas is dissolved in this blood?

_____

iii What is the correct name for blood with this gas dissolved in it?

_____

b These cells enable the blood to carry this gas.
Give **two** ways they are adapted to carry out that function.

1 _____

2 _____

c **i** What is the name of the chemical reaction that every cell in the body needs this gas for?

_____

   ii Write the word equation for this chemical reaction.

_____

_____

d Which organ is responsible for removing the waste gas from this reaction out of the body?

_____

Total

maximum 9 marks

15 Some students wanted to know if drinking cola increased their pulse rate. They all drank a glassful of cola taking care to drink the same amount each to make sure it was a fair test. This was the question they asked:

> Does drinking a glass of cola make your pulse rate higher?

This was their prediction:

> We predict that we will all have a higher pulse rate after drinking a glass of cola than before.

These were their results:

Name	Pulse rate after drinking 200 ml of cola drink
John	65
Sarah	72
Peter	68
James	67
Gemma	69

a **i** Do you think they have the right results to answer their question and test their prediction?

_____

ii Explain your answer.

_____

_____

_____

This was their conclusion:

> From our results we conclude that girls have a higher pulse rate than boys.

b **i** Is this a reasonable conclusion from their results?

_____

ii Explain your answer.

_____

_____

_____

c Why is it always hard to obtain reliable evidence from experiments on living things even if you are very careful to do everything right?

_____

_____

_____

Total

maximum 5 marks

Revision checklist

CELLS

I am able to …

- Describe the structure of plant and animal cells, the things that are the same and the things that are different ☐
- Describe the ways in which some cells are adapted to carry out their special function ☐
- Explain how cells divide to make new cells ☐
- Describe how similar cells group together to make tissues ☐
- Describe how tissues group together to make organs ☐
- Describe how organs work together in the systems of the body, i.e. the digestive system, the reproductive system, the circulatory system ☐
- Recognise the characteristics of living things and explain how the tissues, organs and organ systems enable these characteristics to happen ☐
- Describe how plants make their own food by photosynthesis ☐
- Explain that all living things use food for energy to allow them to move, to grow and to maintain their correct temperature ☐
- Explain how living things release energy from food by respiration ☐

ENERGY

I am able to …

- Recognise the difference between renewable and non-renewable sources of energy ☐
- Describe the advantages and disadvantages of using both kinds of energy source ☐
- Explain how electricity is generated in power stations, and the advantages of using different kinds of energy resource in the generation of electricity ☐
- Describe how electrical current is carried around a circuit ☐
- Recognise the difference between a series and a parallel circuit ☐
- Describe the ways in which energy can change its form, although it can neither be created nor destroyed ☐
- Describe the ways in which energy, including thermal energy, can be transferred ☐
- Explain that energy transfers are never 100% efficient as some energy is transferred at each stage in a form where it cannot readily be used ☐
- Describe how humans and other animals use food as a source of energy ☐
- Explain how the energy content of different foods varies ☐
- Explain how a range of different foods are needed to make up a balanced diet, and why different people need different diets ☐
- Explain how energy can be transferred as sound and as light ☐
- Explain how the frequency and amplitude of a sound wave are related to the pitch and loudness of the sound ☐
- Explain how light is reflected and refracted ☐
- Describe how white light is made up of a range of different colours ☐

FORCES

I am able to …

- Explain how balanced and unbalanced forces affect the movement of objects ☐
- Calculate speed ☐
- Describe how friction acts to oppose motion ☐
- Recognise how air resistance is a form of friction ☐
- Explain how a streamlined shape can reduce air resistance ☐
- Describe the relationship between shape, air resistance and terminal velocity ☐
- Explain how pressure is related to force and surface area ☐
- Explain how gravity affects the movement of objects ☐
- Describe the movement of the Earth around the Sun and the Moon around the Earth ☐
- Explain why we have day and night, summer and winter, and why the Moon looks different at different times ☐
- Describe the existence of a magnetic field around the Earth ☐
- Recognise the ways in which electromagnets can be made stronger ☐
- Recognise the similarities and differences between magnets and electromagnets ☐

PARTICLES

I am able to …

- Describe the behaviour of particles in solids, liquids and gases ☐
- Understand how this behaviour explains physical changes of state such as melting and evaporating ☐
- Describe how to separate one substance from another by a variety of means and to be able to choose the best separating technique in any situation ☐
- Explain what happens when a solid dissolves in a liquid ☐
- Explain the difference between an element, a compound and a mixture ☐
- Recognise the chemical symbols for the first 20 elements in the Periodic Table ☐
- Use those symbols to identify which atoms are present in a molecule of a compound ☐
- Explain the difference between chemical reactions and physical changes of state ☐
- Describe, and give examples of, how the products of chemical reactions can be very different from the reactants with which the reaction started ☐
- Describe chemical reactions in word equations ☐
- Recognise the characteristics of metals and non-metals ☐
- Explain how different metals react with water, steam and acid and use this to describe the reactivity series of metals ☐
- Describe the reactions of metals with water, steam and acid in word equations ☐
- Recognise that rusting and combustion are examples of chemical reactions involving oxygen ☐
- Explain how the pH scale is used to measure acids and alkalis ☐
- Identify the pH of some common substances ☐
- Explain how indicators can be used ☐
- Recognise that acids and alkalis react together to form a neutral compound and how this can be used ☐

- Recognise the three kinds of rock ☐
- Explain how the structure and properties of rocks are related to the process by which they are formed ☐
- Describe the rock cycle ☐
- Explain the effects of physical and chemical weathering on rocks ☐

INTERDEPENDENCE

I am able to …

- Describe the relationships between different organisms that make up a food chain ☐
- Explain how energy is passed through a food chain ☐
- Understand why food webs are more useful in explaining the relationships between organisms than food chains ☐
- Explain why there is always a green plant at the start of every food chain ☐
- Describe the variations within and between species ☐
- Explain the difference between inherited and environmental characteristics ☐
- Describe how plants and animals have adapted in ways that enable them to survive better in their habitats ☐
- Describe the main classification groups of living things and classify organisms according to their features ☐
- Use keys to classify unknown organisms ☐
- Describe how living things compete for resources such as water, light, food and space ☐
- Understand the impact that humans have on the planet and on other species ☐

SCIENTIFIC ENQUIRY

I am able to …

- Identify the variables or factors in an enquiry to be changed, to be measured and to be controlled ☐
- Recognise which is the independent variable and which is the dependent variable ☐
- Explain that all factors other than the independent variable must be kept the same to ensure a fair test ☐
- See trends and patterns in results ☐
- Present results clearly and draw conclusions from results ☐
- Make accurate measurements using the correct instrument and explain why repeating results can make them more reliable ☐
- Obtain information from charts and graphs ☐
- Present information clearly in charts and graphs ☐
- Draw conclusions from data presented in a variety of ways ☐
- Evaluate an experimental procedure and suggest improvements ☐
- Evaluate the reliability of conclusions drawn from experiments and data ☐
- Identify sources of evidence and evaluate that evidence ☐
- Describe the ways in which scientific ideas have changed over time as the available evidence has changed ☐